# A GUIDED TOUR IN A BOOK

Walking and exploring Glastonbury

Glastonbury is a unique place, it can be among other things a place of searching, adventure, exploring, meeting people. People visit Glastonbury for many reasons, some for a few hours, a day, a week, some stay longer.

When I first visited Glastonbury, I remember getting the Tor bus from the car park by the Town Hall to Glastonbury Tor, and then walking down from the Tor via the Chalice Well gardens, and back into the centre of town. Simply because at that time I didn't know how to get to the Tor or anywhere else, the town was new to me and unfamiliar.

Over time I visited Glastonbury many times for many reasons. Most of the first short visits only gave time to spend in the town itself, the Chalice Well, or a walk up the pathway on the Tor, only once venturing slightly further afield. On further visits I began to discover other walks around Glastonbury and slightly outside it as well. Some needing a car to get to them, some in walking distance of/or around the town.

Then after moving to Glastonbury in 2009, I had more time to explore and discover, enjoying the town the pathways and areas beyond. Sometimes I would drive out in the evenings exploring some of the quieter roads finding where they went, but in the daytimes I would either explore by car and walk or walk the area.

The idea came to me, after being asked lots of time on my walks, 'which ways is it to the Chalice Well/Tor?', to put together a book showing the walks around Glastonbury with photographs. So, over several months, I went and walked the walks and took the photographs. However, the biggest challenge was putting the book together. It's a bigger book than I first imagined.

There are many walking books, for short walks and serious ramblers, this is not my intention with this book. Nor is my intention to say how short or long the walk is by miles, time, or suitability. Again there are books and maps for those that prefer to walk this way. After all what may be a long walk to one person can be a short walk to another and what may seem hard to one may be easy to another. Each person is different and has different capabilities.

A walk can sometimes take me 2 or 3 hours, but I may only have walked a short way, spending time sitting, writing, photographing while walking or I may walk further in a shorter time. It also depends on the weather and time of year. To give an idea though the walk to Gog and Magog took me around 2 to 3 hours, that included sitting, stopping, and enjoying the views. The walk from Bushy Coombe to Bulwarks Lane and Bove Town took around 1 hour.

The responsibility for your walk is you. However, be aware that as with all walking you are walking on the land, which can be among other things uneven, muddy, slippery, have unexpected small holes, slopes-both up and down, etc. Some of the walks are on pathways or country lanes and again be aware that they are not always even. Although the lanes are quiet, there can be some traffic, or animals, horses, cows etc. Common sense is needed as in all things! Don't leave any litter and cause no harm.

My intention with this book is to show the enjoyment that can be had on these walks, the views, the feel of the area, not just on the High Street in Glastonbury but pathways the visitor or newly moved to the Town person may not know about and want to explore if they do. It is a guide to lead you to where you may want to go and explore, finding other pathways on your walk if you choose. I hint and you can lead your own way. While following some of these walks you may choose to go other ways you see on your walk. This is not a set guide to follow this path for x amount of miles, its more an opening and introduction to explore. Glastonbury Tor is a good guide while exploring the area around town, I have found if you get 'lost' it's visible from so many places that you can usually find your way back. Some of the walks are near the town centre, some are a bit further away. I also include details of places further away, places I have visited that have either wonderful walks or/and spectacular views, and in most cases, Glastonbury Tor can be seen from them. It gives you more of a view of the landscape and the area around here.

Enjoy.

# Glastonbury High Street and the centre of town

Glastonbury High Street can be lively and busy some days and quiet on others. The shops are a delight of difference from other towns, you may not necessarily get what you are looking for but rather what you need. There are plenty of cafes and pubs to sit and plan what you want to do with your day, where you want to visit etc.

I have started the town walks in this book either from the top of the High Street or outside the Town Hall. There are car parks around if you have a car and most have directions showing you where they are.

Some of the walks can be shortened if needed, for example the Tor Bus goes from the Glastonbury Information Centre near the Town Hall to the Tor, (though it only runs from 1st April to 30th September). If you have a car there are places to park on Wearyall Hill, on the Roman Way or near to the Chalice Well at Drapers or the Rural Life Museum. The choice is yours, but I give directions for all walks in or around Glastonbury as if you are walking from town. Suggested walks further afield I give directions or suggestions as if you are using a car.

Enjoy

The centre of town has quite a few places to visit, including:

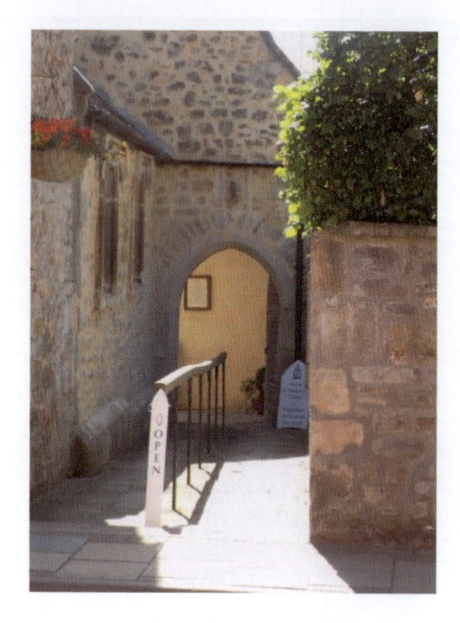

The Magdalene Chapel also known as St Margaret's Chapel (Opening hours vary)

Glastonbury Information Centre, located in St Dunstan's House (opening hours vary through the season)

Glastonbury Abbey
(Admission charge applies) Opening hours vary depending on the time of year.

These places can be found on Magdalene Street.

On the High Street you will find:

The George and Pilgrims Inn

Glastonbury Tribunal

The Tribunal used to be the museum and Information Centre. The Information Centre has moved next to the Town Hall. The Tribunal building is at present closed.

St John's Church

With the labyrinth in the churchyard, which you can walk around. (Gates usually close around 4pm)

Slightly further away on Chilkwell Street/Bere Lane

The Somerset Rural Life Museum.

(Opening hours vary, admission charges apply). There is a car park here (charges apply)

The Chalice Well Trust Gardens, Chilkwell Street

(Admission charge applies)
(Opening hours vary during the year)

And of course, the world famous Glastonbury Tor

Walks around Glastonbury

Willow Walk

Gog and Magog

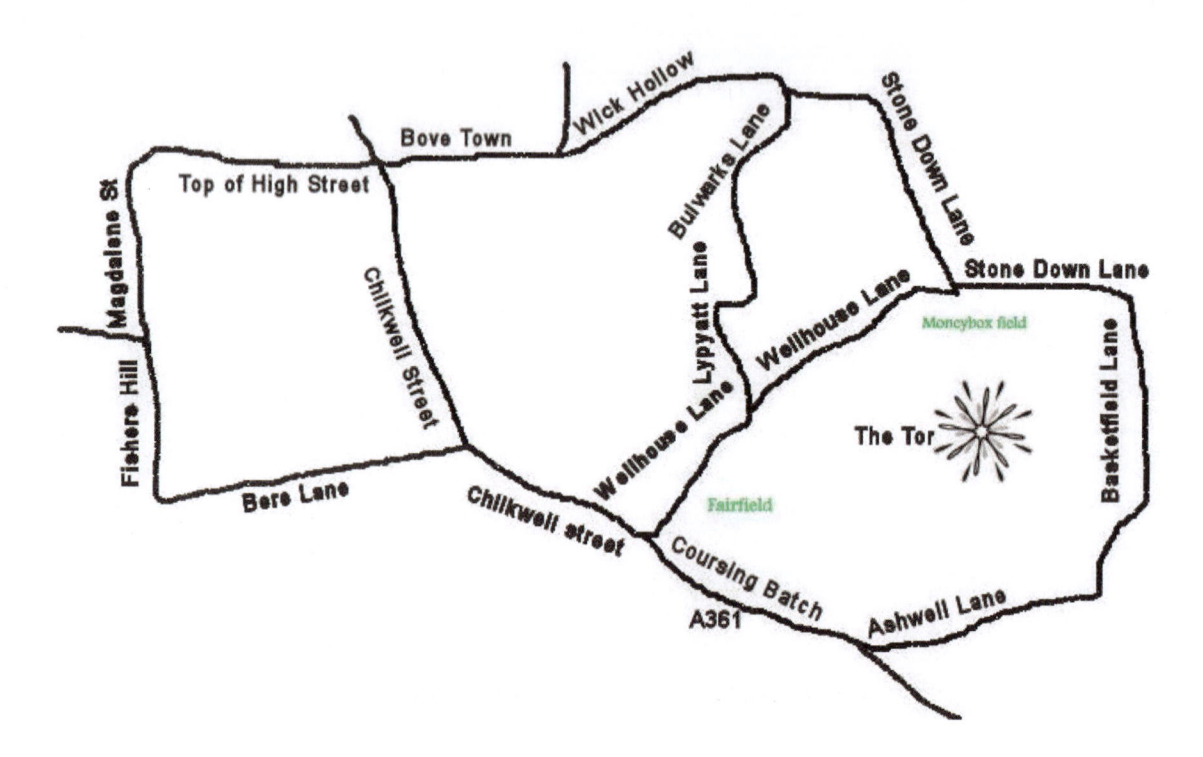

Wearyall Hill

The Avalon Orchard

# WALK 1

## High Street to Chalice Well Gardens and Glastonbury Tor

A walk if you just want to walk to the Chalice Well Gardens or Glastonbury Tor along the main footpaths in town.

# High Street to Chalice Well Gardens and Glastonbury Tor

**From the top of Glastonbury High Street turn right into Lambrook Street,** which then quite quickly turns into Chilkwell Street.

**Keep walking on the footpath until you come to the mini road roundabout. Bear left**, this is still Chilkwell Street.
The path is now higher than the road and has railings.

The Chalice Well Gardens will be on your left further along this footpath.

Just past the Chalice Well Gardens there is a road on the left. (Wellhouse Lane).

**Turn up this road.**

**On the right you will see a pathway, take the pathway up to the top of the Tor.**

# WALK 2

## Bushy Coombe, Bulwarks Lane, Bove Town

This is a circular walk starting and returning at the top of the High Street. It is mainly on the lanes and footpaths and is a good walk for a rainy day if you don't want to get muddy!

**Bushy Coombe, Bulwarks Lane, Bove Town**

**From the top of Glastonbury High Street turn right into Lambrook Street** which then quite quickly turns into Chilkwell Street. **Follow the street pathway until you come to Dodd Lane** (second street on the left) which has a signpost pointing to 'footpath to the Tor'.

**Go up Dodd Lane** look out for the prayer wheels which will be on your right.

**Then go through the small gateway ahead of you into Bushy Coombe.**

**Keep to the pathway up and through the Coombe.** The first part is steep but there is a bench near the top to sit on if you want to sit for a while. There are 3 benches to sit on along the way and you will find spectacular views from 1 of them over the town of Glastonbury.

Depending on the time of year the view will differ through the trees but look out for your sighting of Glastonbury Tor as well as views of the town.

Have a look for the lime tree, also known as Grandmother Lime. It's a beautiful old tree which provides shade from the sun on a hot day. It will be on your left and is sometimes hard to see because the land dips where the tree is.

**Go through the small gateway and follow the lane upwards until you see a pathway and gateway ahead of you.**

**The road leads off left at this point, follow the road and it will take you into Bulwarks Lane.**

**Follow the lane,** looking out for some unexpected views of Glastonbury Tor and the town itself.

**When you come to the end of the lane turn left into Wick Hollow** where you will see some beautiful old trees.

**Follow the lane down until you come to Bove Town, go left down Bove Town and back to the top of the High Street where you started.**

# WALK 3

## Bushy Coombe, Bulwarks Lane, Windmill Hill, Bove Town

This walk starts and finishes at the top of the High Street, taking you on a sort of circular route to Windmill Hill before returning via Bove Town.

**Bushy Coombe, Bulwarks Lane, Windmill Hill, Bove Town**

At the top of the High Street, you will see a church in front of you, have a look at the interesting well stone here and see if you can spot the 'To the Tor' on it.

Then **from the top of Glastonbury High Street turn right into Lambrook Street** which then quite quickly turns into Chilkwell Street. **Follow the street pathway until you come to Dodd Lane** which has a signpost pointing to 'footpath to the Tor'.

**Go up Dodd Lane,** look out for the prayer wheels on your right, **then go through the small gateway ahead of you into Bushy Coombe.**

**Keep to the pathway up and through the Coombe,** there are 3 benches to sit on along the way and you will find spectacular views from 1 of them over the town of Glastonbury.

Depending on the time of year the view will differ through the trees but look out for your sighting of Glastonbury Tor as well as views of the town.

Have a look for the lime tree, sometimes affectionately known as Grandmother Lime, it is a beautiful old tree which provides shade from the sun on a hot day.

**Go through the small gateway and follow the lane upwards until you see a pathway and gateway ahead of you.**

**The road leads off left at this point, follow the road and it will take you into Bulwarks Lane.**

**Follow the lane,** looking out for some unexpected views of Glastonbury Tor and the town itself.

**When you come to the end of the lane turn left into Wick Hollow.**

**Slightly further down Wick Hollow you will come to a bench on your right** set back slightly from the road, there is a footpath sign pointing to your right but don't take this footpath, **go left up the footpath incline,** which takes you above Wick Hollow along a small woodland.

Looking down from here you can see the trees of Wick Hollow and the road beneath.

**Follow the footpath,** you will see Ridgeway Gardens (a small road of houses will be on your left, through the trees and fencing).

**Carry on until you reach the end of the footpath** and a small road appears, this is Sandpits Road.

If you look to your right, there is a stile, don't go over this but if you wish, stop, and have a look at the view towards Wells.

**Turn left from the pathway and go towards the shop at the crossroads.**

Over the road from the small supermarket shop there is a play area and an open area of grassland, this is the mound on Windmill Hill, formerly called St Edmund's Hill.

You can, if you wish, **go over to the mound,** and have a look at the view to the Tor and surrounding area. Windmill Hill or St Edmund's Hill is the only sacred hill in Glastonbury that has been extensively built on.

**Then go back towards the small supermarket shop.**

**Turn right and follow the Bove Town road down, back towards the top of the High Street and where you started.**

**WALK 4**

**Bushy Coombe to Glastonbury Tor
(With options to go to Chalice Well and White Spring)**

A walk starting from the top of the High Street taking you up to the top of Glastonbury Tor, giving you three options for return.

# Bushy Coombe to Glastonbury Tor
## (With options to go to Chalice Well and White Spring)

**From the top of Glastonbury High Street turn right into Lambrook Street** which then quite quickly turns into Chilkwell Street. **Follow the street pathway until you come to Dodd Lane** which has a signpost pointing to 'footpath to the Tor'.

**Go up Dodd Lane,** look out for the prayer wheels which will be on your right, **then go through the small gateway ahead of you into Bushy Coombe.**

**Keep to the pathway up and through the Coombe,** there are 3 benches to sit on along the way and you will find spectacular views from 1 of them over the town of Glastonbury.

**Go through the small gateway and follow the lane upwards until you see a pathway and gateway ahead of you.**

**Follow the pathway through the trees,** beautiful and shaded in the summer months, muddy in the winter months, look out for a view of the Tor if you have not already seen it and some of the apple orchards on the Isle.

**When you reach the gateway go through it into the field, follow the right-hand trackway through the field,** (the Tor will now be in front of you), **until you reach the gateway to Wellhouse lane.**

**Go into Wellhouse lane and turn left, walking up,** (there is a bench at the joining of the roads to sit on and look at the view of the Tor).

**Carry on up the lane,** which is now StoneDown Lane, **until you reach the gateway to the Tor field on your right.**

**The Tor bus stop is further ahead on the left.**

Note: The Tor bus only runs from April 1 to September 30).

**Go into the field,** there is a millennium milestone in the field to your left as you go through the gate. This field is called Moneybox Field.

**Follow the footpath,** at the top of the field you can **either**

**Go left through the small gateway into the Avalon Orchard** and spend some time there.

**Or**

**Go right and follow the footpath up to the top of the Tor.**

If you choose to go into the orchard, it's a lovely place to sit for a while. There are apple trees, sometimes sheep and views out towards the Mendip Hills and its fairly sheltered, though that depends on the way the wind is blowing on the day!

If you have gone into the Avalon Orchard. **You can then either go back through the gate you entered and onto the Tor path through the small gateway to your left.**

**OR**

**You can go through the gate at the top of the Orchard, (to your left as you are looking at the Tor) and then up some steps and onto the Tor path that way.**

**Follow the footpath to the top of the Tor,** it's quite steep in places but there is a bench on the way.

Spend some time on the Top of the Tor. After all you have been walking on it for a while, enjoy the views. Take photographs, sit, walk round, look at the Mendip Hills, the view to the distant sea, usually best seen on a beautiful sunlight evening when the light just catches the water in the distance. This used to be an island, imagine the water all around. See Wearyall Hill in the near distance, Chalice Hill, Windmill Hill, and some of the other hills, the rhynes seemingly dividing the fields.
Enjoy the view, the feeling.

# The Labyrinth

The terraces or grass pathways circling and winding around the Tor are the Glastonbury Tor labyrinth.

The terraces are easier to see sometimes from a distance or at certain times of the year. You can find maps and books on how to walk the labyrinth if you wish to do so. The labyrinth entrance isn't as some think at the top of the Tor but is actually on one side, around a third of the way from the top, marked by an egg stone. The start is again, not at the bottom of the Tor but again, around a third of the way up, near a large stone at the side of the footpath that leads from Chalice Well side.

If you do choose to walk the labyrinth and you are not familiar with it, it would be best to have a guide, whether paper, person, or internet, to show you the way, some of the levels have now slipped and cross over near the bottom and make it difficult to tell which level is which. I have walked the labyrinth once and although glad of the experience and the guides I am in no rush to do it again!

**To return**

**Option 1**

You can then either walk back down the Tor the way you came up, and back through Moneybox field.

From Moneybox field turn left into Wellhouse Lane, when you reach the gateway **further down the lane** (after the joining of the roads) **follow the pathway across the field.**

Then go through the other gate onto the pathway then the lane to Bushy Coombe and back to town.

**Option 2**

If you go back the way you came but instead of going through the small gate into the field carry straight on down the road (Wellhouse Lane), keep walking until you come to the White Spring and outside wall of the Chalice Well Gardens.

**Option 3**

**You can go back down the Tor from the top but by the other pathway,** it looks longer but is less steep than the one you came up from.
(Wearyall Hill will be ahead of you in the distance).

The path leads down into a field, (called the Fairfield) **follow the path down the field, through the gate and then down a darker concrete pathway to the bottom of Wellhouse Lane.**

The wall to the Chalice Well gardens will be in front of you, the White Spring to the right, and the outside access to both the Chalice Well and White Spring water is on this lane. The White Spring on the right of the road, the Chalice Well on the left as you look up the lane.

**If you don't wish to visit the White Spring, turn left at the end of the pathway and then right onto Chilkwell Street.**

If you wish to go to the White Spring it can be visited (opening hours vary), no admission charge but donations welcome when open. You can see in from outside if it is closed, the gates are metal designed and can be seen through.

**If you have walked up the road to the White Spring and outside access to the Chalice Well water you then need to go back down the lane, towards the main road,** it's just a short way.

**Then turn right onto the main road, following the outside walls of the Chalice Well Gardens.** The entrance to the Chalice Well is on your right, opening hours vary throughout the year, (entrance charge applies).

**Carry on the footpath** which becomes higher than the road, (if you have visited the Chalice Well turn right out of the gardens).

You are now on Chilkwell Street, **carry on until you come to a small roundabout,** the Somerset Rural Life Museum will be on your left. (The photograph shows the Rural Life Museum taken from the slopes of Glastonbury Tor).

You can **either carry straight on,** you are still on Chilkwell Street.
The Glastonbury Abbey wall will be on the left and back **to the top of the High Street where you started.**

**OR**

At the end of the high Path, **you can go left at the roundabout onto Bere Lane,** (this is quite a busy road for traffic).

**Follow the path along the road back down into the centre of town,** the road bears right and goes past the local Abbey Park.

**When you get to a small road roundabout, keep going ahead,** this takes you past the Magdalene Chapel on your left and the Abbey railings on your right and **back to the Town Hall.**

# WALK 5

## Bushy Coombe to Glastonbury Tor via Lypyatt Lane

This is a walk up through Bushy Coombe and onto Lypyatt Lane with the option to either go up Glastonbury Tor through the Fairfield or carry on down Wellhouse Lane and back to town.

## Bushy Coombe to Glastonbury Tor via Lypyatt Lane

**From the top of Glastonbury High Street turn right into Lambrook Street** which then quite quickly turns into Chilkwell Street. **Follow the street pathway until you come to Dodd Lane** which has a signpost pointing to 'footpath to the Tor'.

**Go up Dodd Lane,** look out for the prayer wheels which will be on your right, **then go through the small gateway ahead of you into Bushy Coombe.**

**Keep to the pathway up and through the Coombe,** there are 3 benches to sit on along the way and you will find spectacular views from 1 of them over the town of Glastonbury.

**Go through the small gateway and walk the short way until you reach the lane.**

**Turn right and go down the lane** (Lypyatt Lane).

**At the end of the lane turn right** onto Wellhouse Lane.

**Just after you have turned right there will be a large and small gateway ahead of you on your left.**

**Go through the small gateway and into the field** (this is the Fairfield part of Glastonbury Tor).

**Take the grass pathway across the field and then the gate to the left at the top of the field.**

**Follow the pathway up to the top of the Tor.**

See the following option if you don't wish to go through the field and up the Tor on this walk.

**OPTION**

**If you don't want to go up Glastonbury Tor**

**Don't go through the gateway but carry on down Wellhouse Lane.** You will then come to: -

The White Spring will be on your left.

The wall to Chalice Well Gardens will be on your right.

**Turn right at the road junction.**

Chalice Well Gardens are on your right.

After visiting the White Spring or Chalice Well – or not –

**Carry on along the high footpath until you reach the mini road junction.**

**Either carry straight on along Chilkwell Street and back to the top of the High Street**

**Or go right and along Bere Lane, bearing right at the top of the hill back to the Town Hall.**

**WALK 6**

**Bushy Coombe to Gog and Magog**

A longer walk up through Bushy Coombe taking you on the lanes past Glastonbury Tor and then down to Gog and Magog with 2 options to return.

**Bushy Coombe to Gog and Magog**

**From the top of Glastonbury High Street turn right into Lambrook Street** which then quite quickly turns into Chilkwell Street. **Follow the street pathway until you come to Dodd Lane** which has a signpost pointing to 'footpath to the Tor'.

**Turn left and go up Dodd Lane,** look out for the prayer wheels which will be on your right, **then go through the small gateway ahead of you into Bushy Coombe.**

**Keep to the pathway up and through the Coombe,** (there are 3 benches to sit on along the way and you will find spectacular views from 1, possibly 2 of them, depending on the time of year, over the town of Glastonbury).

**Go through the small gateway and follow the lane upwards until you see a pathway and gateway ahead of you.**

**Go through the small gateway and follow the pathway through the trees.** (This pathway is beautiful and shaded in the summer months and can be muddy in the winter months. Look out for a view of the Tor if you haven't already seen it and some of the apple orchards on the Isle).

**When you reach the gateway go through it into the field, follow the right-hand trackway through the field,** (the Tor will now be in front of you), **until you reach the small gateway to Wellhouse lane. Go through the small gateway into Wellhouse lane and turn left, walking up the lane.** (The Tor will be on your right. There is a bench at the joining of the roads to sit on).

**Carry on up the lane,** which is now StoneDown Lane, (there are some disabled car parking spaces on the right), then you come to the gateway to the Tor footpath, which is on your right.

Don't go through the gateway but **keep going until you reach a turning in the road.**

**Take the road to the left,** which is still StoneDown Lane.

**Walk along the lane and look out for three gateways on your left,** two large ones with a smaller gateway in the centre.

**Go through this smaller gateway and follow the pathway,** which is narrow and has hedging either side, **until you reach the gateway at the end. Go into the field.**

You will see a gateway on your left at the top corner of the field, remember the gateway but don't go that way.

**Follow the grass footpath down the field until you reach a hedge with a metal walkers gateway in it. Go through the gateway.** (Take some time to look at the views and turn round occasionally to see the Tor behind you).

**Carry on down the second field, following the grass pathway until you reach a stile** (the Old Oakes Caravan and Campsite will be in front of you as you walk across the field).

**Climb over the stile and turn left,** the footpath sign will say Maidencroft Lane.

Just a short way along on your right, (you may already have seen them from a distance), are the remains of the ancient oak trees Gog and Magog.

(Gog and Magog are the last 2 of an ancient avenue of oak trees which used to run to the Tor).

Spend some time at Gog and Magog if you wish then afterwards you have 2 options (or more if you want to go off exploring).  This book is a guide not a must do!

**To return**

**Option 1**

**You can follow the path back the way you came, over the stile** (The wooden sign will say Paradise Lane and Glastonbury), **back up through the fields until you get to the two small gates at the top of the field.**

**This time take the gate on the right, at the very top end of the field,** not the one you came through before.

**Follow the footpath,** (Paradise footpath) (there are some seats in places along this way, where you can sit awhile and look at the views).

**Carry on until you come to the end of the path.** (The path widens, and it's called Paradise Lane, though it's not a tarmac. The Tor will be on your left).

**Go through the gate onto Maiden Croft Lane.**

**Take the lane in front of you,** which is Maiden Croft Lane. (Maiden Croft Lane also goes off to the right, don't go this way).

**Walk down the lane until it turns into Wick Hollow. Carry on down Wick Hollow,** (look out for some beautiful old trees).

**When you come to the second road junction turn left into Bove Town and back to the top of the High Street.**

## Option 2

From Gog and Magog, which will be on your right, go through the small gateway on the right, the sign says public footpath.

**Follow this footpath, there is another small gateway, go through that and follow the grass path across the field,** (the Tor will be on the left in the distance).

You should see a stile in the trees ahead of you, **climb over the stile,** (this one is quite high on one side as the pathway drops down slightly).

(There is a small stream and woodland where you can spend some time if you wish. It's only small and narrow but quite beautiful and secluded).

**Then cross the bridge over the stream**, there is a stile at one end of the bridge and then another stile just up the banking on the other side.

**The grass footpath goes straight up the field,** (the Tor is still on your left). There were horses in the field when I walked across it. (That's the way the footpath goes, the horses I am told are very friendly).

**Climb over the stile and into the lane,** (there is a small orchard in front of you), **take the left-hand turn of the lane and follow the lane through Paddington Farm.**

(There is a mural on one of the buildings on your left as you pass through the farm).

This is more like a lane than a pathway.

You will see a cattle grid ahead, **carry on around the cattle grid,** there is a sign that says walkers only.

You are now on Maiden Croft Lane, **follow the lane upwards until you come to the top.** It's quite a way but worth it. (There are some stunning views through the trees and hedges along the lane).

**Keep going until you come to the top of the lane,** (the Tor should be visible ahead of you a short while before you reach the top of the lane).

When you get to the top of the lane there are three ways to go, **take the lane to your right** (which is still Maiden Croft Lane).

**Walk down the lane,** it turns into Wick Hollow. **Carry on down Wick Hollow,** looking out for some beautiful old trees.

**When you come to the second road junction turn left into Bove Town and back to the top of the High Street.**

# WALK 7

## Wearyall Hill

A short walk to Wearyall Hill

# Wearyall Hill

**From Glastonbury Town Hall walk past the car park and along Magdalene Street.** (The Abbey grounds will be on the left and the Magdalene Chapel on the right).

**At the mini roundabout carry on up Fishers Hill.** (The Abbey Park will be on your left).

**Cross the road at some point here** and **when you get to the top of the hill take the first road on your right** – Hill Head Road.

**Walk up Hill Head Road.** (There is an interesting sign hanging outside one of the houses). When you come to the top, you will see a layby/parking area and gateway on your right.

**Go through the gateway and go left up the grass path of Wearyall Hill.**

(The remains of the site where the Holy Thorn was are on the hill, it is no longer there but others have been planted in places around the town). There are spectacular views of Glastonbury Tor and the levels of Somerset in the distance).

There are benches to sit on to enjoy the view on different parts of the hill. It's also a good place to take photographs looking towards the Mendips and Glastonbury Tor.

**To return**

**Option1**

**You can either go back the way you came.**

**OR**

## Option 2

When looking towards the town, Morrisons supermarket will be visible at the bottom of the hill.

**Follow the grass footpath downwards toward the direction of the main road.**

**When you get to the bottom go through the gateway and onto the paved footpath.**

**Turn right, Morrison's will be on your left.**

**When you get to the mini roundabout, go left, and follow the pathway along Magdalene Street -**

**And back to the Town Hall.**

# WALK 8

## Wearyall Hill to Brides Mound via the River Brue

A longer walk over Wearyall Hill to Bride's Mound via the River Brue and through fields with stunning views along the way.

# Wearyall Hill to Brides Mound via the River Brue

**From Glastonbury Town Hall walk past the car park and along Magdalene Street.** (The Abbey grounds will be on the left and the Magdalene Chapel on the right).

**At the mini roundabout carry on up Fishers Hill.** (The Abbey Park will be on your left).

**Cross the road at some point here** and **when you get to the top of the hill take the first road on your right** – Hill Head Road.

**Walk up Hill Head Road. When you come to the top you will see a layby/parking area and gateway on your right.**

**Go through the gateway and go left up the grass path of Wearyall Hill.**

**Follow the grass path to the top of the hill and carry straight on along the hill.** There are three seats on the hill to sit and enjoy the views.

There is a gate about halfway down the hill, **carry on through the gate.** There is a seat to sit and enjoy the views here.

**Keep going down the pathway and through the stone divider and down the stops leading onto the Roman Way.**

**On the Roman Way, turn right and follow the road a short way.**

There will be a grassed area with trees and a seat in front of you, on the left fields and walks by the river Brue, ahead the pelican crossing and Pomparles Bridge. The main road (Street Road) is usually busy here, so **go to the pelican crossing.**

You will see a pelican crossing and bridge in front of you. The bridge is Pomparles Bridge (the perilous bridge) and has the River Brue running underneath it.

**Cross the road at the pelican crossing.**

**Then go right** but only for a very short way towards Glastonbury. **Just after the end of the bridge you will see a footpath sign and small gate on your left by the side of the river.**

**Go through the gate.**

**Follow the grass footpath along the side of the river.**

(The river has high banks so is hard to see in places and at certain times of the year, in some places you cannot see the river at all). You may see a road on your left, this is a narrow road and a short cut from Street to Meare.

**Carry on the grass footpath, following the river.** You will reach a gate, go through, and keep going along the footpath.

After a short way on your right, you will see a seat below the grass footpath. (It's a lovely spot to sit and enjoy the views). Glastonbury Tor and Wearyall Hill will be slightly to the right, the chimney from the old Morlands Factory in front of you and Brides mound is in front of you in the near distance.

**You can then either make your way around this field towards the small wooden gateway at the other side of the field.** It is hard to see from a distance.

**OR**

**You can go back onto the grass footpath, turning right with the bench behind you, walk for a short way and go into this next field.**

The Brides Well stone is situated here (the well stone can be difficult to spot in the summer months when the grass is long because it's at the bottom of the banking, however you should see trodden grass down to it from the top of the banking).

**Make your way around the field over to the small gateway to Brides Mound.** This gateway is among the trees and you may see some ribbons or offerings hanging on the trees or blowing in the wind.

**Go through this gateway onto the mound**.

(Brides Mound in near to the town sewerage works so sometimes there are interesting smells blowing in the wind!)

**From the mound you should see an area of new planted trees.**

**Walk to the gate to the right of these trees,** there is/was an information marker board here.

**Go through the gate, turn left, and go through the next gate until you come to the end of the lane.**

**Turn left and follow the way round past a coal/wood yard on your right,** it's only a short way and brings you onto the road which is Beckery Old Road.

**Turn left and walk along Beckery Old Road.**

(This part of Glastonbury is under regeneration and although not the prettiest area of the Isle of Avalon it's an interesting place).

**Follow the Beckery Old Road,** which should be nearly straight ahead of you, Wearyall Hill will be on your right.
There are some old derelict buildings here but also some new buildings as well.

**Follow the road,** it has signs with a car and bike showing 'except for access' plus a cyclist dismount signs. The old factories are here.

**Keep walking ahead, until you come to a road turning, again keep going ahead.**

**You will reach a junction with a sign saying 'Beckery New Road', again keep going ahead along the road.**

This is now Beckery Road.

**Keep going ahead past the industrial buildings until you come to Park Farm Road, which should be on your right.**

It has a no through road sign on it.

**Go down Park Farm Road a short way until you reach the main road and pelican crossing.** A sign says Glastonbury Town Centre.

**Cross at the pelican crossing and go right through the walkway in the wall,** the sign again says Glastonbury Town Centre.

You are now on Benedict Street, (Wearyall Hill and the fields of Tor Leisure will be on your right).

**Carry on ahead along Benedict Street,** see how far along you go until you see the Tor again.

**At the top of Benedict Street cross the road, you are back at the Town Hall.**
Glastonbury Information Centre is next to the Town Hall.

# WALK 9

## Wearyall Hill to Brides Mound via Beckery

A shorter walk over Wearyall Hill to Bride's Mound via Beckery, showing different aspects of Glastonbury.

# Wearyall Hill to Brides Mound via Beckery

**From Glastonbury Town Hall walk past the car park and along Magdalene Street.** (The Abbey grounds will be on the left and the Magdalene Chapel on the right).

**At the mini roundabout carry on up Fishers Hill.** (The Abbey Park will be on your left).

**Cross the road at some point here** and **when you get to the top of the hill take the first road on your right** – Hill Head Road.

**Walk up Hill Head Road. When you come to the top you will see a layby/parking area and gateway on your right.**

**Go through the gateway and go left up the grass path of Wearyall Hill.**

**Follow the grass path to the top of the hill and carry straight on along the hill.**

There is a gate about halfway down the hill, **carry on through the gate,** there is a seat to sit and enjoy the views here.

**Keep going down the grass pathway,** it bears to the left.

**Keep going down the pathway and through the stone divider and down the stops leading onto the Roman Way.**

**On the Roman Way, turn right and follow the road a short way.**

There will be a grassed area with trees and a seat in front of you, on the left fields and walks by the river Brue, and ahead the pelican crossing and Pomparles Bridge.
The main road (Street Road) is usually very busy here, so **go to the crossing.**

You will see a pelican crossing and bridge in front of you. The bridge is Pomparles Bridge (the perilous bridge) and has the River Brue running underneath it.

**Cross the road at the pelican crossing.
Then go right towards Glastonbury.**

**After the Glastonbury, Isle of Avalon sign, take the left turn onto Beckery.**

**Walk along the road,** Bridies Yard building will be on your left, **keep walking until you come to a road on the left.**

**Take the left road and follow the road round, it's not far.**

**Just past the coal/wood yard on your left go right onto the grass trackway.**

**Go through the gateway and then the next gateway and onto Brides Mound.**

On Brides Mound there was/is an information marker board on top of the mound itself.

(Brides Mound in near to the town sewerage works so sometimes there are interesting smells blowing in the wind!)

Spend some time on the mound if you wish then –

**To return**

From the mound you will see an area of new planted trees.

**Walk to the gate to the right of these trees,** there is/was another information marker board here.

**Go through the gate, turn left, and go through the next gate until you come to the end of the lane.**

**Turn left and follow the way round past a coal/wood yard on your right, it's only a short way and brings you onto the road which is Beckery Old Road.**

**Turn left onto Beckery Old Road.**

(This part of Glastonbury is under regeneration and although not the prettiest area of the Isle of Avalon it is an interesting place).

**Follow the Beckery Old Road,** which should be nearly straight ahead of you, Wearyall Hill will be on your right.

There are some old derelict buildings here but also some new buildings as well.

**Follow the road,** it has signs with a car and bike showing 'except for access' plus a cyclists dismount signs. The old factories are here.

**Keep walking ahead, until you come to a road turning, again keep going ahead.**

**You will reach a junction with a sign saying 'Beckery New Road', again keep going ahead along the road.**

**Keep going ahead past the industrial buildings until you come to Park Farm Road, which should be on your right.** It has a no through road sign on it.

**Go down Park Farm Road a short way until you reach the main road and pelican crossing.** A sign says Glastonbury Town Centre.

**Cross at the pelican crossing. Go right through the walkway in the wall,** the sign again says Glastonbury Town Centre.

**You are now on Benedict Street,** (Wearyall Hill and the fields of Tor Leisure will be on your right).

**Carry on ahead along Benedict Street,** see how far along you go until you see the Tor again.

**At the top of Benedict Street cross the road you are back at the Town Hall.**

# WALK 10

## A walk by the River Brue

A walk from the Town Hall, up Hill Head and onto the Roman Way, then down to the River Brue with wonderful views of Glastonbury Tor.

## A walk by the River Brue

Note: This area can be flooded at certain times of the year, especially in the winter and early months and after a lot of rainfall in these seasons.

**From Glastonbury Town Hall walk past the car park and along Magdalene Street**, The Abbey grounds will be on the left and the Magdalene Chapel on the right.

**At the mini roundabout carry on up Fishers Hill**, the Abbey Park will be on your left. **Cross the road** at some point here and **when you get to the top of the hill take the first road on your right** – Hill Head Road.

**Walk up Hill Head Road until you come to the top where you will see a layby and gateway on your right**, this is the gateway onto Wearyall Hill and the grass footpath.

Don't go through the gateway but **carry on down the lane** which is now the Roman Way.

**When you come to a mini roundabout, turn right** this is still the Roman Way.

**Follow the road a short way, keep a look out on your left for a narrower lane**, (sometimes looking slightly overgrown), it has a footpath marker and goes between two houses.

**Go down this lane, there is a wooden gate, go through the gate and follow the grass footpaths**, one goes across the field the other goes along the edge, both will take you to the river.

Glastonbury Tor will be on your left before you get to the river.

Clyse Hole Weir is on this part of the river there is a bridge where you can walk across the water here.

Pomparles Bridge will be to your right in the distance, though you may not see it from this point.
(Photo shows Pomparles Bridge from the Street Road)

**You can then choose to walk along the river in whichever direction you would like to go**, making your walk, short or long.

Note: There are no seats along this walk apart from sitting on the ground.

**If you go left it takes you in the direction of the Butleigh Road.** If you wish, you can cross the Butleigh Road, you will see the footpath sign across the road. You can then carry on along the river for as far as you want before returning.

**If you go right this takes you in the direction of the Street Main Road.**

**To return**

You can then choose to find your own way back or go back the way you came following the grass footpath back up through the field and onto the Roman Way, up Hill Head and back into town.

(If you do go left along the path in the direction of the Butleigh Road I would recommend you walk back again to the weir and then the way you came. The Butleigh Road is very busy and narrow and there are no footpaths).

# WALK 11

## A short walk by the River Brue

This is a short version of the River Brue walk for those with a car.

# A walk by the River Brue (short version)

Note: This area can be flooded at certain times of the year, especially in the winter and early months and after a lot of rainfall in these seasons.

If you have a car and want a short walk by the River Brue, there is road parking on the Roman Way near the Street Road.

To get there, **go out of Glastonbury towards Street and just after the Red Brick Building (which will be on your right) look out for a left-hand turn.**

**Take the turn left into Roman Way and park.**

**You should see two walks, both on the same side of the road.**

One in the direction of the houses on the corner of Roman Way. This walk is alongside a small waterway. **Go through the small gate and follow the grass footpath.**

The other walk can be found in the corner through the trees.

**Go through the small gateway to walk alongside the river.**

It's a lovely place to walk and also has views of Glastonbury Tor, Street can be seen on your right.

Note: There are no seats along this walk apart from sitting on the ground.

You can walk as near or far as you wish.

# WALK 12

## The Willow Walk

I've called this walk the Willow Walk but it is actually part of the cycle/walk way out to Ham Wall on the Somerset Levels and now also called the Bittern Trail. Quite a few people asked me to put the walk in this book.

# Willow Walk

I've called this walk the Willow Walk but it is actually part of the cycle/walk way out to Ham Wall on the Somerset Levels now called the Bittern Trail and quite a few people asked me to put the walk in this book.

There are two ways to get to this walk, this is probably the easiest way.

**From Glastonbury Town Hall, walk down Benedict Street** (Benedict Street is between Mocha Berry and Heaphy's Cafes) **to the very end**. The road bears right near the bottom but carry on ahead. The Tor Leisure park will be on your left and views of Wearyall Hill behind it.

**Go through the gap in the wall and cross the road at the Pelican Crossing.**

Just ahead of you on the other side of the Pelican Crossing **go onto Park Farm Road. Walk along Park Farm Road**, it's only a short road. **Then go right and across near the mini roundabout**, you should be crossing a small stone bridge. **You are now on Porchestall Drove Road**.

**Walk along Porchestall Drove Road** and **keep going until you come to a road turning right.** (There is a signpost in blue saying 'Peat Moors Visitor Centre) pointing right.

(This photograph was taken just after turning right and looking back)

**Turn right onto this road**. (Glastonbury Tor will be on your right).
**The road is called Middle Drove.**

**Walk along until you come to a large metal industrial looking green gateway on your left.**

(There is a sign in blue across from the gateway saying Peat Moors Visitor Centre).

There is a lovely picnic area called Amy's picnic area in the field with seating and tables should you wish to stop for a picnic).

**Go through the gateway onto the track**, it follows the waterway in a meandering path through some trees and then some willow trees.

The part of the pathway with the willow trees is quite atmospheric and beautiful.

This walkway is now part of the Bittern Trail and will take you to Ham Wall and the Avalon Marshes (around 4 miles there) should you wish to walk that far, otherwise it's a lovely short walk up to the river bridge and back. It's up to you how far you choose to walk.

## The longer Willow Walk

I've called this walk the Willow Walk but it is actually part of the cycle/walk way out to Ham Wall on the Somerset Levels and now part of the new Bittern Trail. Quite a few people asked me to put the walk in this book. (This is the longer way)

# Willow Walk (longer way)

**From the Town Hall go right and towards the market cross then walk down Northload Street.**

Northload Street is quite a long street so **keep going until you see a large road roundabout at the end** (Manor House Road will be on your right).

**Keep to the footpath on the left near the roundabout and follow the path round until you reach the pelican crossing.**

**Cross at the pelican crossing and follow the footpath/road through Northload Bridge.**
(This is a small group of houses).

**At the end of this short road go left**, (there are now large gates in the field on your left, this is Herbies Field and was bought by the Town Council) **you have to walk on the road for a short way, there is no footpath.**

You should see The Isle of Avalon Campsite on the road which bears right. Don't go that way but **stay on the main road**, the road goes over a small bridge, this is a busy road to Meare so be very careful.

**Just after you have walked over the bridge there is a road to the left, go down this road.**
This is Dyehouse Lane, the waterway will be on your left along with a view of Glastonbury Tor.

**Walk along the road,** there will be a small pond on your right then further along the road, **just before the road curves left there is a large and small gateway on your right.**

**Go through the small gateway into the field and follow the grass footpath, through the fields.** Glastonbury Tor will be behind you.

**Follow the path ahead,** going through another small gateway with a small bridge into the next field **until you come to another small gateway.**

**Go over the small gateway onto the lane and go left.** This is Middle Drove Road.

**Keep walking until you reach the industrial looking green metal gateway on your right.**

It's not far. Glastonbury Tor will be on your left.

**Go through the gateway** and follow the willow walk as far as you wish.

There is a lovely picnic area called Amy's picnic area in the field with seating and tables should you wish to stop for a picnic).

You can either return the way you came from here or follow the return directions (below) for the short Willow Walk and make it a circular walk.

**To return to Glastonbury from the Willow walk**

**Go back through the metal gateway**

**Turn right onto the road,** (Middle Drove Road).

Glastonbury Tor will be on your left.

**Keep walking until you reach the road junction.**

**Turn left towards Glastonbury.**

After a short way, a timber yard will be on your right.

When you come to the end of Porchestall Drove Road, bear right across the mini roundabout onto Park Farm Road.

At the end of Park Farm Road, cross the road at the Pelican crossing.

Go through the wall walkway onto Benedict Street and walk along Benedict Street and back to the Town Hall.

## Suggested walks in areas near to Glastonbury with views of Glastonbury Tor

There are many places to walk in the area surrounding Glastonbury and it's not that far from the coast either.

A car is recommended to get to these walks because some are not on bus routes. I have given detailed directions for some of the walks but others just suggestions for places to visit and for you to find your own directions there.

Glastonbury Tor from Ebbor Gorge

# Somerset Levels
# RSPB Ham Wall at Ashcott

You will need a car to go out to the levels.

From Glastonbury Town Hall, go left.

At the mini roundabout go right (towards Street)

At the B&Q roundabout go right (towards Wells).

At the next roundabout go straight ahead (towards Wells).

At the next roundabout go left (the road out to Meare, B3151)

Stay on this road, (the river will be on your right but above the road, you can see the banking but not the river)

When you reach Meare look out for the Fish House on your right. This used to be part of Glastonbury Abbey and is the only surviving monastic fish house in England.
There is a small parking space, or you can park on the road nearby to have a look at the Fish House if you wish. Although the Fish House is not open you can walk around outside or if you wish the keys are available from Manor House Farm which is at the opposite end of the field to the Fish House.

If not or after you have visited the Fish House, carry on through Meare past the old school house on the left, it has a bell tower on it and the church on the right.

Look out for Ashcott Road, it will be on your left, not long after the old school house.

Turn left and follow Ashcott Road, it's a narrow bumpy road built on peat with passing places.

Keep going until you reach the Railway Inn which is on your left.

The original car park for Ham Wall is on your right just over the bridge near the Inn.

The new Ham Wall car park is slightly further up the road on your left.

(The new car park closes at different times during the year, the old car park stays open all the time). Car parking charges apply.

From these car parks there are different walks on the levels, bird hides and seats. From some places you can see Glastonbury Tor in the distance. All the walks here are flat, some can be muddy as they are grass pathways, but some are gravel or board pathways.

It's a beautiful area to explore and truly get a feel of Glastonbury being an Isle in the distance.

Glastonbury Tor from Ham Wall area of the levels.

Ham Wall area of the levels – sunset on water

The pathway from Ham Wall old car park towards Westhay

# Somerset Levels

## Shapwick Heath National Nature Reserve – Westhay
### (Known as the Sweet Track)

You will need a car to go out to the levels.

From Glastonbury Town Hall, go left.

At the mini roundabout go right (towards Street)

At the B&Q roundabout go right (towards Wells).

At the next roundabout go straight ahead (towards Wells).

At the next roundabout go left (the road out to Meare, B3151)

Stay on this road, (the river will be on your right but above the road, you can see the banking but not the river)

Carry on through Meare (B3151) towards Westhay

At Westhay take the left turn onto Shapwick Road

Carry on along this road until you see The Avalon Marshes Centre on your left.

You can park here or carry on along the road for a short way until you reach a bridge, just after the bridge there are two parking laybys on the right and left of the road.

From here there are various walks on the levels. Some are on gravel paths, some on boardwalks on the wetter marsh part and some on built up tree bark covered paths.

You can also see a reconstruction of the ancient Sweet Track here.

And have a chance to walk on it!

It's a beautiful area. From the bird hide near the water at the end of one of the pathways, Glastonbury Tor can be seen.

Note: In the winter months the starlings come to visit and stay, giving spectacular displays near sunrise and sunset.

Note: It can be very busy in this area at these times both at the Ham Wall and Westhay areas, with lots of visitors going to watch the starlings.

# Coombe Hill Woods

## Coombe Hill Woods is situated off the Street to Somerton Road

Coombe Hill Woods is a lovely place to go walking in the woodlands with some walks giving spectacular views across to Compton Dundon. From the Admiral Hood monument views of Glastonbury Tor can be seen.

Address for your satnav is Coombe Hill Wood, Reynald's Way, Glastonbury, BA6 8TP

From Glastonbury take the road towards Street. Just after Pomparles Bridge there is a roundabout.

Take the first left turning on the roundabout. There is a sign saying, 'Welcome to Street' (Signpost says Somerton B3151)

At the next roundabout go straight ahead (Signpost says Somerton B3151)

At the traffic lights go straight ahead (B3151)

Keep going until you see the brow of a hill and crossroads coming up.

At the crossroads turn left – the road is called Reynald's Way. Keep going along the road for quite a way until you see a car park sign on your right. (The car park can be difficult to see until you are nearly upon it.)

Park in the car park and choose your walks from there.

The car park is in the woodland itself and there are plenty of walks and paths to follow here.

Some of the walks are on gravel pathways, some on grass pathways or forest pathways. There is a short circular flat walk from the car park but most of the other walks are on rougher pathways and hilly terrain.

This is a place to explore, get the feel of the woodland, the trees, and the beautiful scenery around. You can make the walk as long or short as you wish.

The view from Coombe Hill Woods towards Compton Dundon

Glastonbury Tor can be seen from the Admiral Hood monument, part of one of the walks in Coombe Hill woods.

## A walk on a ridge with views of Glastonbury Tor

## Walton Hill, situated on the Cockrod Road

From Glastonbury take the road towards Street.  Just after Pomparles Bridge there is a roundabout.

Take the first left turning on the roundabout.  There is a sign saying, 'Welcome to Street' (Signpost says Somerton B3151)

At the next roundabout go straight ahead (Signpost says Somerton B3151)

At the traffic lights go straight ahead (B3151)

Keep going until you see the brow of a hill and crossroads coming up.

At the crossroads turn right – the road is called Cockrod.

On the right you should see a Youth Hostel and car parking for Ivythorne Hill, there are some walks here, but I haven't walked this part. If you wish you can have a walk from here.

Keep driving along the road until you see a small car park layby on the left of the road, it's on the high ridge of the hill.

Park in the layby.

There are some short walks here.

You have option of going either down and through a small woodland.

Or

Along the ridge with views of Glastonbury Tor one way and Compton Dundon the other.

As with Ivythorne Hill Walton Hill is part of the Polden Hills range.

**Ebbor Gorge and Deer Leap**

Ebbor Gorge can be approached from either Wells or from Priddy.

From Glastonbury take the road to Wells, Somerset.

At Wells take the A371 Wells to Cheddar Road, following signs to Wookey Hole.

At Wookey Hole, go past the caves and after around a mile bear right up Deer Leap.

The car park for Ebbor Gorge is on the right.

There are various walks at Ebbor Gorge, through the gorge and woodland or you can make it a short walk from the car park.

It's hilly terrain in parts and some of the pathways are rough but it's well worth the climb, if you are able, go up to the viewing area of the Gorge for the views with Glastonbury Tor in the distance.

Equally if you want a short walk and view of the Tor, just from the car park (on the right with the car park entrance behind you) there is a grass pathway with seating and views of the Tor. Further down this pathway on the left, you can see into the Gorge.

You can make your walk as short or long as you wish.

To get to Dear Leap car park.

To get to Deer Leap, either carry on driving up the road after you have seen Ebbor Gorge car park or if you have parked in Ebbor Gorge car park, turn right up the hill.

Deer Leap car park is further up the road on the left.

Deer Leap has a picnic area and seating.

It also has walks along the ridge with stunning views both towards Glastonbury Tor one way and the coast the other way.

Or you can walk down into the valley.

This area has nature reserves which are lovely to explore.

Again, it's a place where you can either sit and enjoy the views or make your walk as long or short as you wish.

# Brent Knoll

Brent Knoll is an Iron Age hill fort which can be seen from miles around, the motorway and main roads run near it.

It is approximately 15 miles from Glastonbury, if you would like to visit rather than directions here, I suggest you check out the website and directions to get to Brent Knoll.

It's within travelling distance of Glastonbury by car and is located roughly halfway between Bridgwater and Weston Super Mare.

Looking inland from Brent Knoll

Once you get to the hill, there are pathways to follow, and it is a climb up to the top but it is worth it!

There are stunning views and again you can see Glastonbury Tor from the top along with the coast and the motorway!

Looking towards the coast from Brent Knoll

# Brean Down

Brean Down is a promontory off the coast at Brean, it is at the very end of the road from Burnham-on-Sea to Brean, literally! You can go no further than the National Trust car park at Brean.

The beach and Brean Down are free at all times.

Car parking

Although the Down is open all the time the NT car park entrance gate is locked at different times during the season, it closes earlier in the winter than the summer.
Note: You can exit but not enter after the entrance gate is closed. Check the National Trust website for time of closure before visiting. Payment charges apply for non NT members. Blue badge holders and NT members park free.

There is also a private car park just after the NT one, opening and closing times vary for the season, payment charges apply to all.

There is also parking on the beach (on the left) just before you get to the end of the Down, again opening/closing vary for the season and charges apply.

Brean Down is the setting for the novel 'The Sea Priestess' by Dion Fortune. You can have an easy stroll on the beach though beware of the sinking, muddy sands in places.

The Down itself looks steep from the bottom and it is! It is a steep walk to start with, but I found that the road, although longer was easier to walk up than the steep steps but the choice is yours.

It's well worth climbing up onto the Down itself and walking along to the hill fort which is around a 3-mile round walk. Though allow yourself some time to do this it can be a longer walk than realised and also can depend on the weather and what it is doing on the day!

The Down is a very atmospheric place, especially the old fort at the end of the Down, so allow time to enjoy and experience.

And yes, Glastonbury Tor can be seen from the Down itself!

The sunset's from Brean Beach can be spectacular.

I hope you have enjoyed your 'Tour in a book' and spent time walking, experiencing, and enjoying the places mentioned as much as I have in creating this book for you.

Enjoy

Vanda Lloyd's other books and photography can be found on: -

Website:  https://lloydbux.wixsite.com/vanda-lloyd

Facebook page – Avalon Dreaming, Glastonbury

All rights reserved.
No part of this publication may be reproduced, stored in a retrieval system, or transmitted in any form or by any means, electronic, mechanical, photocopying, recording, or otherwise, without written permission of the author.

Words and Images © 2021 Vanda Lloyd Revised Edition

Printed in Great Britain
by Amazon